SHE HAS A NAME

SHE HAS A NAME

Kamilah Aisha Moon

Four Way Books
Tribeca

Please direct all inquiries to:
Editorial Office
Four Way Books
POB 535, Village Station
New York, NY 10014
www.fourwaybooks.com

Library of Congress Cataloging-in-Publication Data

Moon, Kamilah Aisha.
[Poems. Selections]
She has a name / Kamilah Aisha Moon.
pages ; cm.
ISBN 978-1-935536-34-5 (alk. paper)
I. Title.
PS3563.O5614S54 2013
811'.54--dc23
                              2013004426

This book is manufactured in the United States of America and printed on acid-free paper.

Four Way Books is a not-for-profit literary press. We are grateful for the assistance
we receive from individual donors, public arts agencies, and private foundations.

This publication is made possible with public funds from the National Endowment for the Arts

and from the New York State Council on the Arts, a state agency

and from the Jerome Foundation.

[clmp]

We are a proud member of the Council of Literary Magazines and Presses.

Distributed by University Press of New England
One Court Street, Lebanon, NH 03766

Contents

Notes

Author's Note: This is a "biomythography" in poems—a term coined by Audre Lorde, based on a larger family narrative. I can only speak for and as myself definitively.

This book is dedicated to my beloveds: James, Carolyn, Niya, and Lakie

BORDERLESS COUNTRY

1 in 150 now, this glitch
in babies poised to unlock the world—
these daughters and sons of poets,
store clerks, salesmen, singers,
CEOs, janitors, actors cast
into this permanent script.
Souls we love turned
like the faces of flowers thrust
toward a rogue sun.

We are the earth we walk; what seeps
here? Is the air fighting back?
Is the water slowing baskets down,
sending them back upstream? Are we changing?
Dear God, are they here
to tell us, in a way we cannot ignore,
that we aren't changing
fast enough?

Autism, the one-drop rule for minds
we strain to understand, the catch-all
phrase that drops kids off
at nowhere,
at you don't exist once you turn 18,
at native tongue of one,

at white-knuckled translation cobbled
through touch across time,
at marquee symptoms
while causes lurk,
at beauty that demands
seas of patience.

What about that drug I took once? Vaccines?
Some karmic boomerang I don't remember
throwing, its stealth return.

1 in 150 apples of somebody's eye.
1 in 150 "my baby."
1 in 150 now, a new child
breathes, private riddles
of our loving strapped
on many backs.

BREACH

It seems
the most special of beings endure
harrowing beginnings.
The covering physician didn't know
her body's history. He treated Mama
with less grace than a laboring
mare—
almost dragging her off the table,
and she had no choice
as he ripped my sister
into this world.

ONE THEORY

They wail, holler
from a place leagues-deep
within. Rock
back and forth for hours,
staring at patterned walls.

They see something—
it blizzards
their brains.

NAMES

Heirlooms more sacred than shedding quilts
or a tarnished pocket watch,

they crown babies ripening
like new verses
in the same epic song.

(Parents)

Our child's mind is on lease to her
from the stingiest of lenders.
You can't tell this when her tiny lips
break open, gourds of joy,
her mouth a toothless shrine.

"If your voice could overwhelm those waters, what would it say?
What would it cry of the child swept under, the mother
on the beach then, in her black bathing suit, walking straight out
into the glazed lace as if she never noticed, what would it say of the father
facing inland in his shoes and socks at the edge of the tide,
what of the lost necklace glittering twisted in foam?"

—Adrienne Rich, from "An Atlas of the Difficult World"

(Parents)

Each year we depreciate.
We tell ourselves
that if anything must spoil,
let it be us. She's worth a million urges. Hope lies
in the new; everyone knows this.

(Father)

The last thing
I ever wanted was to let her
down. I held her high
in the boughs of my biceps,
until her legs began to grapevine
around mine.
She didn't wriggle
like my older girls did,
restless for ground. No. Lord, no.
Please. Not my baby girl, not the one
named after Mama, gone.
Mouth carved just like hers, like mine.
What could I have done?
Held her as long
as any father's strength could stand
her growing weight.
What next?

(Mother)

I watched the backs
of college girlfriends trailing off
to mobile lives. I watched them
until they were blips.

Ours was a sacred exile
then. Waterfalls
of words between us.
Silhouettes in love, tending our own.
The hours, clouds
floating past—beds in the sky
where rain slept.

—

I often wake up dizzy,
the sun mocking us
as it douses her face.

My husband says nothing,
his kisses shallow.
What we don't say
we eat.

(Father)

My chromosome limps
in her blood stream.
The proof—
years later, my brother's son
scales this cliff.

I'm not allowed to say
I don't want to pay
what she will cost us.

I'll work myself into pulp, withhold
my tongue and practice nothingness.
Cockroach logic: if I don't move,
I'm not really against this wall,
back gleaming in harsh light.

I won't hold my wife's hand and skip words
like stones. I'll become a dike of a man,
fall asleep in front of the TV
nightly until I burst.

(Father)

In my arms, she was safe
from sharp corners,
shocks. She wasn't "delayed,"
a problem to solve again
and again, or resign to having.
The world is aberrant, not us.

The doctors, my wife, and others spoke
of what was to come
and what wasn't.
No matter how hard I focused,
I couldn't hear them.
Couldn't bear to understand.

LOVE IS A BASIC SCIENCE

They ran tests.
Looked for reasons
she learned like molasses.

She didn't like to be touched.
Walked on her tiptoes
everywhere, a braided
ballerina in flip-flops or Keds.
Our way of walking
a plodding, ill-fitting gait
that continued to confound.

It wasn't extraordinary in our minds
to love her,
to let her know,
holding on until she squeezed back.

ME AND MY FRIENDS CIRCA 1981

We liked sitting on the swings
eating 25-cent frozen fruit cups
and spitting out the Styrofoam
Depending on the mood of the day
we'd roll around on our blacktop
skating rink or ride to Fleming's Market
on banana-seat bikes with plastic streamers
in the handlebars
At least half of us walked around
wearing constant Kool-Aid mustaches
and fresh knee scabs
We played hide-n-seek before
everyone discovered the fun
of hiding in pairs
and it was always cool
to make a sidewalk gallery
Henry O. Tanners, chocolate
Matisses and Picassos armed
with Crayolas and pastel chalk
would spread out on Lenore St.
to express ourselves
Making our mark on the inner city
in something other than blood.

FLASHES FROM THE FAMILY ALBUM

Baby girls peeping from car seats, carriers,
strollers, over shoulders,
and riding hips.

Birthday cakes,
lopsided, pointy hats.
A missing diaper waving like a flag
from a giddy one-year-old's fist.

8-track soul serenades,
waltzes with Daddy in the living room,
tiny sneakers bouncing with each step.

Scooby-Doo wading pools,
frilly Easter dresses.
In PJs rifling through gift wrap piles,
shampooed heads in bathtub poses.
In bright pink shorts sets
running across green fields,
climbing jungle gyms.

Mickey Mouse hats,
backpacks, and rain slickers.
Paddington Bear vandalized
with black marker whiskers.
Red-nosed snowmen-makers
in full winter gear.

Afro-puffed, Easy-Bake sessions
on the back porch.
Snaggle-tooth smiles.
Sundresses and rainbow sandals
outshine the difficult
in the camera's eye.

PINWHEEL

Supermarket scenes and other public displays
ended with kicking and screaming,
Mama undone.

The yelling,
crying, and refusing
to walk,
legs dragging
like a life-size rag doll.

This sea of sound, smell,
and color I took to
dolphin-like, engulfed her—
crashing against the rocks
of her mind's shore.

Do we HAVE to take her with us outside this time?

She made us look bad.
I had no other way home—
purples, blues, and reds
spinning in my head.
I wanted to twirl free
and not be undone.

ACHILLES TENDON: WAR AT 3PM

Playground henchmen trailed me,
nipped at my heel.

Nerf-ball taunts whizzed
by my ear. I headed toward dinner
and being tucked in—away
from jellybean rivalries
that wouldn't mean much
once we traded arithmetic for algebra,
wiped salty words
off my brow.
Until a few yards later,
YOUR LITTLE SISTER IS A RETARD
sliced me.

I went down fighting.
Took them with me
in a hail of fist-fire.

Except I rose.
Her honor saved,
gauze and hydrogen peroxide fizzing
in broken skin.

(Middle Sister)

For most of elementary school,
people thought we were twins.
At a glance, she "passed"
next to me.

Linger; we become distinct.

My eyes sparkled green.
I had words, my mind mostly in a world
I made up long before I knew why
I needed my own.

Her eyes shimmered brown.
She made random noises
that reminded me of TV static,
shook her head "No" at questions
I couldn't hear.

I was mad when she arrived.

But I got over it soon enough
and began to get it, began to bare
my new teeth at those
who ignored my near-twin.

MEMORY IN THE PARK

Swinging was the closest thing
to flying then. Pushing off
a little harder each time, we sailed
above the monkey bars
and the first tier of maple limbs.

I remember the day when she swung
back and forth unattended—beaming
as giggles rode the wind shotgun with her.

I saw her pleasure naked.
I saw it.

STIGMA

She hated that short yellow bus.

The sentence felt each day
it pulled up sighing
to McMurray Jr. High's curb,

delivering her to locker-lined halls
full of metallic, 7th-grade teeth.

SPECIAL ED TEACHER

I have the population
others don't want.
How does one look out
into a room of leg braces
and mute stares expecting
to find sparks, a "high-functioning" one?

I register them with the Special Olympics,
bring in Oreos and Hi-C for the Christmas party.
Xerox their initial progress reports
(some years old)
to re-sign,
tell them what a joy it is
to have them in my class.
I see them out to the short yellow buses
and go home. I stopped crying after
the first year, stopped trying
after the second.

They never felt like lies
until I was caught.
This is the first parent to hold me to them;
most give me credit for smiling
in the class picture.

FREQUENCY: AN ULTIMATUM

Who are you, dammit!
Make yourselves known—

    Spooks and haints
        that speak only
            to her,
  unholy chorus
        stalking the shoulders
            of my parents' third angel.

  Dog-whistle voices
        take her away mid-sentence;
            brazen cackles
                bar her from sleep.
    Headsets on the nightstand offer
            DJ chatter and quiet storm melodies
                just white enough to drown them,
    so she can sneak into REM
            unfettered by strange music.

        What do you say? Why can't I hush you
        when she bristles at your whispers?

  Decoding crests and troughs
        that wash past our ears,

I must somehow tune into this station
    on the mental dial where
        she listens to heavy air
            my comprehension can't weigh.

I wish my love-static interfered
        with magnetic tongues
           luring her from herself.

      Find another mind or else—

PECKING ORDER

Jostling for high perches
is for the birds

Such a small victory to look down on your

Niece
    Cousin
        Church member
            Classmate
                Neighbor

Those smug
beaked glances
nick her spirit

PROM NIGHT

Perennial high school fantasy—
ball gown evening for some,
a nightmare
of mice and pumpkins for others.

A black-sequined maiden; rhinestones
parody sparkling eyes.
A tenderfoot prince; debonair
from the inside out.

They danced in the spotlight.
Classmates from the regular courses
(who seldom speak) paused in awe.

Long past the bewitching hour,
she added her picture
to those on our piano,
a memento of her chapter
in the fairytale.

ASSEMBLY REQUIRED

To the man at Black & Decker who harassed her daily

8 a.m. sharp, you snap
Part A into Part B.
The conveyor belt brings
more resentment.
There are quotas to fill
as you wait for the dull ache
in your lower back to tell you
it's lunch time.

The ham sandwich and MoonPie
don't nourish. You are pissed working
next to someone like *her*. Heartburn
turns you into a swearing, shoving fool
full of sour laughter.

You are careful to use the urinal
farthest from the bank of mirrors; later, you drag
long and hard for 10 minutes every 2 hours,
leaning against weathered brick.
She comes home acrid
as your smoke every evening.

Go ahead—
talk loud and bully
the clawless one.

This man talks about me real bad, Ish
I just try to be nice
don't know why he acts like that

Sometimes they don't speak
It's like I'm not here

I don't like the job it's too easy and boring
I can move out with y'all, go to college and get a car
and have a good time
I miss you

NO ROOM FOR GRAY

Between is a hard place to live.

She shuns wheelchairs and
mongoloid faces, mad that her mind
will fight to keep her
quarantined
from her own car, yard,
babies.

You are. Or you are not.
You're sick. Or you're well.
One thing. Or another.
But it's never that simple
like breathing should be.

Between is a hard place to live.

Each morning she stretches
her fingers toward a life
just out of reach,
and grudgingly squeezes
into a seat at a table
that bumps her knees.

(Mother)

Sometimes I wish she didn't know
as much as she does. I hate knowing
that she imagines another life, too.

What kind of boys would my left-handed
fashion maven have brought home?
What campus would we have lugged boxes to?
She fixates on news, gossip, sings
songs of all kinds . . . enjoys a good cocktail.
Her peach cobbler and casseroles
taste better than mine now.
I collect clues like foreign coins
she can't spend.

AIRPORT SCENE AFTER HER FIRST SOLO VISIT

She wanted to fly like us, experience
peanuts and ginger ale at 35,000 feet.
Rent metal wings
and hurtle through the sky—
free to defy
Autism's gravity and simply be
the passenger in seat 13E.
She was coasting,
a look-ma-no-hands smile
resplendent on her face.

My fear
shortened her ride,
as I led her by the hand
to the front of the line,
telling the attendant
to keep watch
that she is *different.*

"Why did you do that to me?!"

Bruised but standing, she turned
to exit through the gate—
her flight home
a lesser altitude.

It was hers.
She had this choice
behind curtained bliss,
Dad's chest full on the other side
as her tapered hand
pulled the lever.

No matter how wide
the final margin,
a lone ballot
never counted so much.

(Ish)

College is not Canaan, Sis—
not a promised land
to independence,
to normal.
Not etched in stone.

Come down from your Mt. Nebo
of longing, discover your own
route to paradise.
We'll meet you there.

AFRICAN DANCE CLASS RECITAL

She moves to the djembe,
hips heeding blood rhythms.
Her sweat-soaked face shines,
an amber moon. Wren-like
feet flutter as limbs fly
on the drums' demand.

Dance beautiful one
Reach for the sky
and sway to Earth's floor
Feel the groove little sister
Dance 'til you can't dance no more

Everyone takes turns
in the center of clapping hands,
ululations caught
      and thrown back
from the corners of the room—
village call and response for the original
Soul Train line. Body rotating
double-time, she makes
a complete revolution,
pausing
      on the downbeat
to a thunderous "Ashé!"

Dance beautiful one
Reach for the sky
and sway to Earth's floor
Feel the groove little sister
Dance 'til you can't dance no more

FRISSON: REMEMBERING JAMAICA

Turquoise salt bath, mango and banana trees, steamed fish,
rice and peas, ackee. Fluorescent insects land on the lids
of cups. Head swimming with new scents, I think
of goats and my friend's braids under a shawl
of fuchsia blooms. White lightning
and ginger wine, stars whizzing by at 50 mph
on narrow, unlit country roads, drunken hand
reaching out the rear window to touch them. Oh,
the beauty of brothers, the astounding range.
They cared for us like kin, their laughter filling
the humid night above the hip-swiveling beats of roadside DJs,
the lazy wooden arms of a shanty's ceiling fan—streams
of people flowing in and out, sweet bulges pressed
against backsides, the whoosh and tingle. The man who
had me hemmed up next to his beat-up Toyota
after a dozen *No's*, his rum-doused rap
in my ear. Fresh coconut water tastes
like tears. Steel-drum tongues, chiseled natty boys
with ivory teeth somersault into waves. Skirts
wear women there, caress eggplant thighs…the gloss
of cleavage, napes of necks call like cantaloupe.
A boy with threadbare sneakers shoos flies on the corner,
cup waiting for change. Rainstorms naked in the sun.
The furious flush from my womb in this kind of heat
moonrays across the mélange of burnished skin.

The anklet of whitefish my friend wore in the sea,
the gentle suck at my fingertip.
The conch dying lovely on the oatmeal shore.

My mother listens, dreams. Hangs
the sandy postcard above her head.

DIRECTIONS

Don't drop your sister. Ever.
Especially when I'm gone. I don't believe
you care as much as I do. I want to, but
how could you, really?

And should you? Gorgeous wind
in your sails. But I need you
to carry her, to want to carry her.

Hold her hands on both sides, crossings ahead
swift and brutal. Never let her out of your sight,
like years ago in the park, in the mall, at the movies.
Like after church on the lawn when your father
wasn't looking, didn't correct those who only asked
about the first two. Promise me she won't inhale
the ammonia smell of group mess halls,
wince at the prying fingers of hired help.

Promise me, girls.

(Middle Sister)

We know "watch your sister" means forever.

She gets this too—checks in with everyone,
wanders room to room. Flicks the light switch off and on
at shutter speed, her panic signal.

I'm sorry I take too long
I don't mean to be quiet
I want to say it

SORRY

I failed to notice
the vacant chair,
spotting you
in a corner, talking to yourself.

Days I've lost patience,
spouting pronged, icy words.
I got so carried away!

Buried moments when
I've forsaken you—for instance—
your graduation-night dinner I skipped
to see a concert.

OUTBURSTS

Long-suppressed shouts
gallop through the house

Calling her name or asking
"Who are you talking to?"
quells the stampede
for a spell

After years of reigned tongue
unbridled words break
through her mind's gate
bucking against fate

(Mother)

Cocooning her became everything.
Cocooning means agreeing
to become a shell.

After cancer, recurrence, cells hobbled
by chemo that has since been banned, side effects
becoming front-and-center effects,

we share a phantom cord, now a two-way
lifeline. She tethers what otherwise
would float apart.

(Ish)

Mama, as my hands look more and more
like yours, I want to use them—
use them to gather orchids and zinnias
to give you now
rather than bittersweet petals
sprinkled on mahogany.

I watched you through
a cracked bedroom door
sobbing on the bed
with pantyhose around your ankles.
Dinner still on time.

(Middle Sister)

Dad only brings his shadow home.
Ish can't beat up the newer bullies alone.
Just got my first corporate job, my own place.

I am afraid
but more terrified of her not knowing
different walls, any other air.

We don't look alike anymore.
She's starting to look too much
like what's left instead of what's ahead.

I want to give her the space
to look like herself.

POSSIBLE SELF-PORTRAIT

Making do
with what is available,
she paints a face in tangerine.
Cobalt eyes colossal, electric
Muted thoughts brighten.

WALLET

When I was 18, I found your old wallet
in a drawer. I eased your freshman ID
from the dark slit, smiled at the country hunk
on the hairy lip of manhood
staring back at me. You appear brooding,
but those margarine eyes
cooked a deep brown tell another truth.
Stuck to the other side, a photo booth
shot of your uptown girlfriend.
I have her nose.

Daddy, you're fading;
but, there is still sheen. Snapped
and tucked close, you unfold
on occasion—glimpses
of stray, ancient receipts.

Out of pocket
in your own house, you live
in the sanctuary. Member
of every committee, your voice
soars through hymns, gospel
that wrings out the soul, hangs
sinners up clean and whole
again. The robe hides
everything that sags. Here,
your sacrifices win praise.

At home, glory isn't as clear.
Tearing in places, you brace
for each crisp, new loss—
and now so do I, your firstborn
stitching things together,
carrying you with me
everywhere I go.

WEEKEND TRIP HOME

I finally relinquish the right-corner seat on the couch,
after her pacing and silent deliberation. I am in her seat
and why didn't I already know that? I am derailing
the reversed schedule of sleep, routine midnight TV.
She clings hard to the familiar—gets dressed exactly
the same way every time, each step done at least twice,
three times. She clings hard to the remote control's
promise to deliver, not me. Maybe
she thinks our love endangered, canopies
her heart—wary of letting me or the light of day
back in. I wish she were still afraid of the dark.

(Ish)

Waving, they stand behind the screen
as they always have, sacred sentinels.

When did it happen?
The soul dry-rot, the end of heavy breathing, the loss
of their first names? Their bones and the arthritic dogwood

limbs brace against each other in the yard, wavering
in January wind without blooms. Each visit home frays me,
the price I pay for being able to drive away.

WATCHING A WOMAN ON THE M101 EXPRESS

You sit in a hard, blue seat, one
of the ones reserved for the elderly
or infirm, a statue of need. Your mouth

open as if waiting for water or medicine, as if
mugged mid-sentence, or some ice age hit
right after terrible news.

Oblivious to the metro's bump and buck,
to the toddler begging in Spanish to be freed
from her stroller, to my ogling, you sit

embalmed, racooned, or moosed. You have
the kind of eyes that never quite close,
even in deepest sleep, lids

an undersized t-shirt that leaves belly
exposed. Tears navigate moles, veteran
swimmers of your creek-bed face.

I can't stop looking. You can't get over
whatever has happened, so shell-shocked
that birds could land and roost. I want to ask—

just so you know someone
is paying attention, but not enough
to know what ravages. It's rude

to stare. I'm from the South, a suburb
where Grief pulls the shades first,
stays home if indecent. But

your sorrow struts four rows down
from me, strands you an astronaut
on some distant, undiscovered moon.

Bodies to your left and right read papers,
nap, send text messages. You sit in a hard,
blue seat, mouth open. I study the pink

of your jaw, and wonder if you'll come back
before your stop comes.

TO A JAMAICAN SURVIVOR WITH LOVE

Bless your reflection.
Float on currents
back to yourself,
back to peace,
back to the flavor of curried goat dancing
on your tongue.

Seek the sun,
sweet daughter of Maroons—
until dragged into the depths
by God's blue, wet fingers,
the memory stops breathing.

Do not let this cripple you—his sin
is not your cross.
Stand on sinewy legs and walk, sister—
fluff your hair back into place.
Find the eye, begin to heal.
Weather this hurricane.
You, a sturdy-petaled bloom
beneath howling sky.

DRESSING DOWN

to Shirley Q. Liquor

When you're gay in Dixie,
you're a clown of a desperate circus.

Sometimes the only way to be like daddy
is to hate like him—
hope your brothers laugh
instead of shoot,
wrap a Confederate skirt around your waist.

You traded glamour for nasty tricks—
dethroning your mammy's image for dollars
that will never cover so much debt,
unraveling years she lost
loving you for a living.

BLUES BOP FOR SONNY

1/24/01, native son of Kansas City

It didn't matter if the stage was crowded or it was just
him, a guitar, and an amp. Yellow man strumming
a jazzy blues that never amounted to much green
(playing behind Bird, it's hard to be seen),
he conjured the house and the streets where he grew up
and the friends he had that didn't survive.

I wondered why I cried that way—
his soul plucking the strings.

I basked in the residual light of Sonny's day.
Nothing left for his children, his plot, he gave
all he had—something in his songs whispered
he was about to go home.
He growled a moving lullaby
about owning up and getting by.
His hands shook
as the last note faded.

I wondered why I cried that way—
his soul plucking the strings.

After the weather, KMBC broke the news.
Flashed a brief clip of silver hair, water
brimming his eyes. They mentioned Sonny Kenner
used to be here like it was nothing—
like his fingers had worshiped rosewood frets
all those years for no reason.

I wondered why I cried that way—
his soul plucking the strings.

REQUIEM FOR A CLOSE FRIEND

Tonight, I mourn the conch
atop the bookcase.
Examining its shellacked, unnatural luster—
muscle scraped clean
like watermelon from the rind.
No more two-part harmony and fingers sticky
with wide-eyed love,
just blood rebounding inside
my aging shell.

I'm good for this, slipping my heart
into the wrong palm. I pray soon
that I'll be too good
for this.

These birds won't let me sleep
under sun, she won't let me
under moon.

Come soon, fantasy
I can touch. Come back to self,
so I can steal away,
harriet myself free

over the cobblestones,
past the marionette dolls laughing
in their display cases.

TO A CAMELLIA BLOSSOM

I saw your pretty head lying
beneath the bush. Without
thinking, I kneeled
and cradled you, petals sighing
into grateful palms. Beauty face down
is an abomination. Why
must you suffer the weight
of early perfection? Your vividness
lifts me, lifts all. I wanted
to hold you. Just like that.
Until. I know this kind
of blooming well, to be
so lush, insides so swollen with life
that what was meant to hold you up
can't. I wasn't meant
to hold you, yet here we are
on this stray, brisk day in April
trembling and fulfilled, unlikely
and true. Before I knew what
to call you, I reached and imagined
season after season. Unmoored.

PORTRAIT AT 34

A lover called my face
a Sahara, traced its dunes.
A woman I don't know
blew kisses the other night
meant to hurdle my shoulder,
but I let the mime of her lips confetti me.
Daffodils are on my window sill,
being their flagrantly yellow selves—
I am jealous. I am round
and mysterious, faithful
like my sister in the sky.
A range of sepia freckles slopes
down the left side of my back,
a glimpse of the leopard.
There is the serpentine spine,
the stomach's soft pages of flesh.
Mountainous woman with debutante
hands and feet smooth as limes.
Teardrop breasts, feasts waiting.
Thank you bones, thank you valves.

THE DAY YOU BECAME A PARENT WITHOUT ME

Wasted batch of lover's moonshine,
This blood is old—
Inside the roar of news,
My womb-jug empties.

Dusk sets fire to the porch,
To what was us.
Honey—
Go bathe your son.

GOING UNDER

"*I remember clearly, all those years ago, that my friends onshore didn't understand what was happening to me. They thought I was laughing, but I was screaming . . . they thought I was playing in the surf, but I was trying desperately to keep from drowning. No clue. They just smiled at me and waved.*"
—Desiree Simons

A way to drown on land
is to flood the veins
with sugar & salt until
elephantine ankles
can't lumber another step,
& yes, like Lot's wife, looking back
will do it, looking back until
you lose all color & crumble,
dissolve into the human sea.

Only you will know what
happened, & the death
certificate will lie, blame
some organ's failure.
Your frantic hands will be
misconstrued, lampooned.
Your hungers smothered
in broth that might make
someone else strong someday.

The marooned on rafts
must sip the poison
keeping them afloat, pray
for rescue. What's your
excuse, feet flat
upon earth, flailing
inside your eyes? But they
don't see, don't notice
when it begins or ends.
*We all leak, that's not
a clear sign.* So what
you've learned not all shores
are solid, not all breathing
is living. *These waves
knock us all down.*
No two drownings
look alike.

Shaking their heads, they'll say
you no longer look like yourself,
even after seeing you
every distended day, bloated hour.
They passed you by often & still
didn't know—swearing that, when mouthed,
the words look the same,
help and *hello.*

NOTES ON A MASS STRANDING

I.

Huge dashes in the sand, two or three
times a year they swim like words
in a sentence toward the period
of the beach, lured into sunning
themselves like humans do—
forgetting gravity,
smothered in the absence
of waves and high tides.

II.

[Pilot whales beach themselves] when their sonar
becomes scrambled in shallow water
or when a sick member of the pod
heads for shore and others follow

III.

61 of them on top of the South Island
wade into Farewell Spit.
18 needed help with their demises
this time, the sharp mercy
of knives still the slow motion heft
of each ocean heart.

IV.

Yes—even those born pilots,
those who have grown large and graceful
lose their way, found on their sides
season after season.
Is it more natural to care
or not to care?
Terrifying to be reminded a fluke
can fling anything or anyone
out of this world.

V.

Oh, the endings we swim toward
without thinking!
Mysteries of mass wrong turns, sick leaders
and sirens forever sexy
land or sea.
The unequaled rush
and horror of forgetting
ourselves.

EULOGY

for Joy Lianne Moon

Women break water, and we come. Joy came, and what needed to flow
from her did. Songs, stories, love until her lungs filled with fluid and
she floated from us. Her family—the close ones and the drifted ones,
the blood ones and the borrowed ones—came and flooded church
rafters with hallelujahs for her breath, the gong of 28 springs. Aisles
wet with yearning for our daughter/sister/auntie/cousin turning
into shore. Her late father's insoluble hand helping her cross over.
Something keeled far inside when I heard, saw her sealed lips. Yet once
we came together, what a sea of heartbeats we made! Nuclei calling
to each other, noses and cheek bones whispering, *I remember* and *we
belong.* We knew after the doves batted their wings, white lashes across
the iris of peace, everything petty and pointless flew. When eyes break
water, what is reborn? I could almost hear her laugh as long-standing
damns burst. She is a saint of light now, and I claim this morning
breaking clouds and window panes as her new smile. Breaking as
blessing. Why do we forget this has always been the way?

TAILSPIN

They didn't plan on perishing like this.

Somehow, between the blurring of wings, nesting,
settling on branches that snapped
like twigs, a tumble began.
Their black bodies plunge
through a gape in the side
of a crumbling house.
What else can they do but stare
at the rotten, growing mouth
in the side of the tiny shack that swallows
lives?

Inside, the wife rouses.
She hears their cries thin like the hours,
talons whispering final rites.

She clamors into the phone
while her grown children sit
on the other end of the line without words,
summoning God.
She shrieks at her husband, "Things are dying
inside of our walls!"
"I know," he mutters. "I know." He fought tailspin
for years, still remembers flight.

For awhile they thought
they could holler themselves back into the sky.

THE VULNERABLE LEADING THE VULNERABLE

We worry over
their safe passage
through tomorrow,
that dusky hole.

We pray in cars at stoplights,
on the couch, during holiday dinners
and visits to group homes.
We whisper over the caskets
of parents, as we close
bedrooms doors at night
to keep them
from the ugliness
we face.

We send for guardian angels—
please—sweep down in case
our love isn't
enough.

DUST

Don't move this dust—
my grandmother's
scratched upright,
older than all of us,
has always anchored
this corner. Unplayable,
tuned to scales
that can't exist,
now a weight keeping
yesterday's pages
from flying away.

Everything's moving,
turning into things
we don't want or recognize.

Don't budge our world
or move this dust,
don't remind that
eventually, everything
goes slack
and mute as these keys
decaying golden-brown
in the mouth of her piano,
stringed mausoleum where
we prop our framed pasts.

Sometimes we don't want
what's best,
we just want what was,
for better and worse.
Often all we have
are banged-up blessings.

Please, don't
move this dust
that has danced in this air
for thousands of mornings,
our mingled skins
glitter caught in sunlight.

A SUPERWOMAN CHOOSES ANOTHER WAY TO FLY

woke up again parched from a dream
full of old water, the only urgent tide
in me lately. eddies of sweat,
promise perishing in each exhale.

i matter too why didn't i believe i matter
more than an unblinking, shadowed eye
that refused to look at me with love?

perched on the edge of a day
that could be owl or ostrich—
wise flight or kicking dust,
i pray for wings that sprout beyond
my body if i must be
out of proportion, that my angers
rinse away into the drain
and i'm not driven mad by small
crawlings all over and through me,
by what has branded me
for the rest of this life.

it's always a choice, the angel spoke-sang,
to be stronger than what pulls
us down. let these night sweats
rain a salty hope, despite waking up
full of old water with the flaked mouth

of a sharecropper at dusk.
why stay thirsty when
many draw from my well?
why settle for shacks when i own
a sprawling, rambling heart?

in the bushes, a cat wails
like a woman forced
to defend something precious.
i toss my crumpled sheet
like a discarded cape
and rise, shoulder blades
aching to split open and bloom.

NOTES

This section is difficult to write. . . it has to be contained, but to quote Whitman, "I contain multitudes," and multitudes of people have loved me and guided this work into the collection you are holding. . .

Martha Rhodes and Four Way Books—for the eyes, great care, and support. For saying *yes*, thank you.

Laure-Anne Bosselaar Brown, Jericho Brown, Toi Derricotte, Cornelius Eady, Nikky Finney, Suzanne Gardinier, Joan Larkin, Dennis Nurkse, Natasha Trethewey. Thank you for your expertise and generosity.

A few of the communities I've known: Sarah Lawrence, Cave Canem, Hallmark, LouderArts, Vermont Studio Center and friends, Paine College, Affrilachian Poets, Community-Word Project, Voices UnBroken, My Sister's Room, Sister Circle, Hume-Fogg, Seay Hubbard UMC, Nashville Poetry Arts Scene circa 1993-1996. Thank you.

Amanda Ash, The Anatol-Hurt Family, Yolonda Baker, Derrick Barnes, Kaveh Bassiri, Elana Bell, Natalie A. Bell, Tara Betts, Remica Bingham, Melissa Bolden, Roger Bonair-Agard, Gina Breedlove, Bill Brown, Vinie Burrows, Roohi Choudhry, Holly Clark, Ama Codjoe, Brian A. Courtney, Pat Daneman, Natalie Diaz, Amie Doyen, Camille Dungy, Nicole Terez Dutton, Shannon Effinger, Natasha Ria El-Scari and family, Melissa Febos, David Flores, Krista Franklin, Erik-John Fuhrer, Joanne Gabbin, Stephanie Pruitt Gaines, Guy LeCharles Gonzalez, Nanya Goodrich, Stacey and Franciska Graham, Ellen Hagan, Tina Harris, A. Naomi Jackson, Marcus Jackson, Tyehimba Jess, Amanda Johnston, Quincy and Nina Jones, Martin Kirby, Michele Kotler, Jacqueline Jones

LaMon, Lisa Langford, Peggy Lee, Natalie Lewis, Monique Lucas, Tony Medina, Nina Angela Mercer, Alison Meyers, Dante Micheaux, Carolyn Micklem, Sarah Micklem, Chloé Yelena Miller, Donna Mollo, Maya Pindyck, Tonia Poteat, Lynne Procope, Alice Quinn, Hila Ratzabi, Bushra Rehman, Dee Roof, Victoria Sammartino, Sonia Sanchez, Lani Scozzari, Evie Shockley, Audrey Smith, Linda Staten, Aissatou Sunjata, Marva Stewart, Preston Mark Stone, Alarie Tennille, Anastacia Tolbert, Sharon Valleau, Renée Watson, L. Lamar Wilson. Thank you for your friendship, kindnesses, and opportunities.

Cara Brown, LaShonda Barnett, Jennifer Pickett Frasier, Aracelis Girmay, Candance L. Greene, Melissa Griffiths, Lindsey Horne, Tayari Jones, Ron and Shirley Lewis, Diane Maloney, M.P. Moon, John Murillo, Mendi + Keith Obadike, Kevin Robinson, Brad Thomas, Samantha Thornhill, Anthony Thornton and family, Dierdra Zollar. Rachel Eliza Griffiths. Thank you for staying close.

All of my Moons, Franklins, Ealys, Furtados, Cains, Thomases, Halls, Jeffries…so many names, so little space here.

Deepest appreciation for all of you!

ACKNOWLEDGMENTS:

Agnes Scott Literary Journal, Connotation Press, The Feminist Wire, jubilat, Kansas City Star, Lodestar Quarterly, Lumina, Mosaic Magazine, Regrets Only, The Ringing Ear: Black Poets Lean South, Sable, Sou'wester, Split This Rock Poetry Blog, Storyscape, Temba Tupu, and *Torch Literary Journal.*

Kamilah Aisha Moon's work has been featured in several journals and anthologies, including *Harvard Review, jubilat, Sou'wester, Oxford American, Lumina,* and *Villanelles.* She has taught English and Creative Writing at Medgar Evers College, Drew University, and Adelphi University. She has led workshops for various arts-in-education organizations in settings as diverse as libraries and prisons. A native of Nashville, TN, Moon received her MFA in Creative Writing from Sarah Lawrence College.